ABOUT THE AUTHOR

Munich - Bo:
Geneva - Tel . ...

Lucia Gruber is an independent designer, stylist, trend setter and former senior design leader of a Fortune 500 company. She holds a Master of Arts in Design from the University for the Creative Arts of London, a Bachelor of Arts in Communications & Graphic Design and a certificate in Interior Design from the New York School of Design. Having spent most of her professional life in diverse metropoles across the world, Lucia is known for combining her inspiration from integral societal and cultural change with her approach to combine beauty with function.

Lucia is a firm believer that our quality of life unquestionably depends on the environment with which we surround ourselves. She currently resides in Prague, Czechia with her husband and 2 children.

i

For Giulia & Stella

May you always be grateful, dream larger than life and remember the stars are within reach – just listen to your heart!

Lucia Gruber

THE ULTIMATE HOME OFFICE DESIGN GUIDE

Maximize your productivity
in 5 easy steps

AUSTIN MACAULEY PUBLISHERS™

LONDON • CAMBRIDGE • NEW YORK • SHARJAH

Ordering Information

Quantity sales: Special discounts are available on quantity purchases by corporations, associations, and others. For details, contact the publisher at the address below.

Publisher's Cataloging-in-Publication data

Gruber, Lucia
The Ultimate Home Office Design Guide

ISBN 9781685623326 (Paperback)
ISBN 9781685623333 (ePub e-book)

Library of Congress Control Number: 2023922071

www.austinmacauley.com/us

First Published 2024
Austin Macauley Publishers LLC
40 Wall Street, 33rd Floor, Suite 3302
New York, NY 10005
USA

mail-usa@austinmacauley.com
+1 (646) 5125767

Book Design by Lucia Gruber
Cover Design by Lucia Gruber

Cover Photography:
Interior Design: Sisalla Interior Design
Joinery: Plane Architectural Joinery
Photography: Tess Kelly Photography

I have to start by thanking my amazing husband, Joe. From the love and support to making this possible in the very first place: he was as important to you holding this book in your hand right now as I was. Love & gratitude - always.

Next, I would like to thank Giulia, Stella, Vroni, Kathi, Florence, Ingrid, Fanny, Verena, Leah, Jenny, Christina, Megan, Isabell, Pascaline, Wendy, Lia, Nancy, Olga, Sophie, Andreana, Armando, and of course Higgi and Sepp for all of your never-ending, unconditional encouragement, support and kindness – your hugs and smiles, your great expertise, critical thinking, patience and inspiration this would have not been possible.

Great thanks also to all the amazing photographers, designers contributing so beautifully and of course the editors for their hard work – we celebrate all your dedication & magic!

And, last but not least, of course: my parents, because you can never thank your parents enough for everything.

CONTENT

ABOUT THIS BOOK

The idea to write this book was originally born when I moved into my first apartment in Brooklyn, NY during my beginnings as a designer. On a limited budget and with very little space to deal with, I was wondering how to transform my small nook into a place of living with space for my passion projects and the ability to work from home - yet I could not find any great advice!

During the pandemic the corporate working world was catapulted into a home office crisis: first, people struggle to deliver their business's needs all of a sudden from home without clear guidance available. Now, as corporations understand the financial benefits the part-time-integrated home office brings, working from home simply remains. However most are still not aware what influence our surroundings can have on us and our productivity.

So I decided to step up and fill this gap: Based on data from surveys, behavioral science studies and design expertise, I created this 5-Step Design Toolkit to guide you through the optimal home office setup without breaking the bank. Once you apply it to your working space, you will be able to deliver your business needs more effectively as well as simply LOVE to "go to work" again every day in your home.

ENJOY

INTRODUCTION

CONGRATS - YES, REALLY!

You are very fortunate to be able to work from home. And with this Guide, you made the first step in the amazing direction of being able to fulfill your business's needs in the most efficient and pleasant way possible.

Did you ever wonder why large firms like Microsoft or Apple invest so much into their corporate offices – which turn out simply stunning? Exactly: Because one's environment does influence one's productivity!

I will explain in a few easy steps how you can use Interior Design Principles in combination with behavioral science in your home office to optimize your work–life balance and maximize your effectiveness.

You will simply love going to work.

NOW LET'S GET STARTED

LOVE MUST BE
ALL AROUND

Actually, before we get started, two more things worth mentioning:

Every design choice should make you feel happy and excited! This will be most important to maintain your continued motivation and deliver your best work. Therefore, only choose to do or buy things that visually appeal to you. This is also further explained in the STYLE section.

A second aspect to consider: This book mainly shows the most common home office task needs, which are currently desk work on a laptop/computer; however, the overall guidance is flexible to be applied to any residential working space needs.

DO
SURROUND YOURSELF WITH THINGS THAT MAKE YOU HAPPY – FROM THE PENCILS TO THE SCISSORS.

STEP 1
SPACE

LOCATION, LOCATION, LOCATION

YOUR MOST IMPORTANT DECISION

Why? If you don't have enough space for your needs, you won't be able to work effectively – the good news, most of the time, you do not need a lot of square footage. And of course, you need to make sure you minimize distractions – or else you simply can't focus.

SO FIRST determine which tasks you need, read through the chapter, and take page 38/39 to go on a location hunt through your house.

EXAMPLE CHECK LIST (depending on your task needs)
- o   Minimum space +X m2/sqft
- o   Privacy
- o   Desk Surface (can be expanded)
- o   Electricity (could be added)
- o   Light (can still be enhanced – but ideally natural)
- o   Internet Access
- o   Video Conference suitable background

The final need does fully depend on your business demands, tasks, and personal preference, after all, but this is a starting point.

DO
DEDICATE A SECLUDED SPACE AWAY FROM DISTRACTIONS ▷

HOORAY - I HAVE A SPARE ROOM

Amazing – this is really special and perfect for a home office!
Let's get started: First, take a piece of paper and a pencil and draft a list of all the furniture pieces you would like to have in your office. Then simply head to page 39 to draw a rough outline of the shape of your room in a simple geometric shape and place all the pieces inside it. Just use simple squares and circles and try different options.
HERE ARE SOME IDEAS:

HOW ABOUT A PROMOTION?

A desk placed in the middle of the room will simply make you feel like you just got upgraded to the corner office!

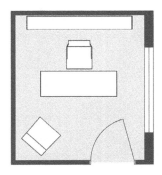

DO

Require a lot of shelving for storage? Perfect – the desk placed in the middle of the room will free up your wall. A floor to ceiling shelf will maximize your space and also make the room feel taller.

DO

If you require a lot of working space, a table extending around the corner along two walls is a great option to increase the desk surface.

HELP - I NEED TO USE MY GUEST ROOM

Fantastic – you have a guest room! Of course, you can have the best of both worlds! Let's go for it: Ideally, you use a convertible sleeper couch or a daybed in combination with your work space and voilà – you can be most productive and still have your guests sleep over! There is not enough floor space for everything? Use a murphy bed and make the bed disappear for daily business!

DO
SLEEPER
COUCH
◁

Or alongside
a guest single
bed

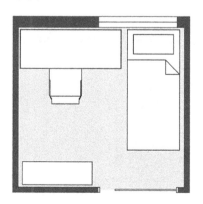

DO
MURPHY BED
◁ ▽

HELP - I FEEL LOST IN MY OPEN FLOOR PLAN

There are various ways to separate your office space visually in your open floor plan so you can feel more grounded in your space. The easiest: You can use a different color palette for your office area. Another great way is to install walls creating a new room, which also adds to more privacy.

DO
INSTALL WALLS
TO CREATE
A NEW ROOM

DO
SEPARATE THE
AREA WITH
A DIFFERENT
COLOR OR DECOR
SCHEME.

HELP - I HAVE TO SETUP MY OFFICE IN MY BEDROOM

Likely, the last thing we want is to physically sleep in the office and mentally remain in our business mindset with all the to-dos and challenges. If your bedroom however, is the only space you have, we can still make it happen in a way that allows you to doze off to sweet dreams and forget about the workday.

BUT HOW?

OUT OF SIGHT OUT OF MIND

The key will be to place your workspace in an area that will be out of direct sight when you lay in bed. Our gaze naturally will lead towards the end of the bed; therefore, the office space makes the most sense off to the side around the headboard area.

DO CREATE A PRACTICAL, YET BEAUTIFUL WORK AREA SIMPLY BY INSTALLING SIDE-TO-SIDE SHELVING AT AN OPEN WALL NICHE ALONGSIDE THE HEADBOARD.

DO
ARRANGE THE
WORK SPACE
ALONGSIDE
OR BEHIND THE
HEADBOARD.

▽

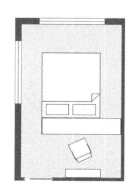

HELP - I THINK
I ONLY HAVE SPACE
IN THE BASEMENT

You won't have any natural light? Also this is not a real problem, but it will be crucial to set up the lighting properly to avoid the feeling of a dungeon you just want to escape as fast as possible. With the right lighting plan, you can create and simulate a natural daylight atmosphere and compensate for the lack of windows.

See the STEP 4 Lighting Section for more details.

HELP - MY HOME IS TOO TINY FOR ANY OF THE IDEAS SO FAR

If you live in a shoebox and can absolutely not dedicate enough permanent floor space to your home office – well you can still create a flexible and functional dedicated workspace. A fold-out desk or even converting a built-in closet or shelving is a great way to open your office in an instant and make it disappear again just as fast with minimal floor space needed. The only watch out here is to make sure you install correctly to make sure safety is given.

DO
CONVERT
A CLOSET ▷

DO

Install a fold-out desk – ideally with storage built-in already.

There are many different types of fold-out or floating desks...the key to the right choice here is to understand how much desks surface you will need and how much storage. But there is definitely an option for every taste and style.

HELP - I WILL HAVE CLIENTS VISITING

The key is to offer comfortable seating in an environment that feels professional. It is recommended to plan the space and furniture for at least two visitor chairs and make sure you know upfront how many people will join you.

Make sure you keep your office clutter free, which means: Everything in this room needs to have a real home – see more in the 'Organization' section!

Fresh flowers will add an extra professional touch. A pen and paper ready for the client, in case they forgot, will finish up the successful setting.

DO

A freestanding desk that enables face-to-face seating for three + allows for a professional setting. Make sure there is privacy for your clients.

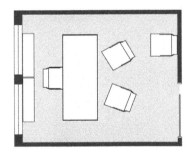

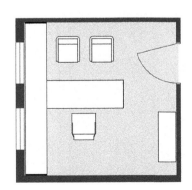

EVEN
MORE
IDEAS

HALLWAY

An option if you know enough privacy will be guaranteed.

NOOK

Nooks are the best hidden secrets in the house. Often you have never even noticed them yet, nor the potential they have to become your new home office.

BUILT-IN CLOSET

Can become magical wonderlands – open them and enter a new room – sliding doors are a practical space saver and a style décor opportunity at the same time.

Side-to-side shelving creates an easy yet great looking working area as well as storage. ◁

STAIRCASE

Staircases are your elephant in the room – your new office space that has always been there but never talked about. ◁

AVOID COMMON MISTAKES AND PITFALLS

CLUTTER

Make sure everything has a home, so you can easily clean up at the end of the day.

HOW? BE HONEST!

What do you have and what do you really need? You have 38 different reasons why you need all of this? That's great!

Now let's find an appropriate, beautiful home for each item.

HIGH TRAFFIC
AREAS

Such as entry-ways
and kitchens
tend to attract people
and motion, which
often is unexpected.

▷

OUTDOORS

The varying
temperatures of an
outdoor/shed/garage
located working space
won't offer enough
secured working
conditions unless
you invest a lot in the
proper setup.

▷

NOW IT'S YOUR TURN - STEP 1

TAKE A TAPE MEASURE, PENCIL + ERASER:

- Complete the Location Checklist.
- Measure your space.
- Sketch the approximate shape of your room.
- Add doors and windows
- Try some arrangements for your desired furniture pieces – you cannot draw very well? No worries at all really – simply work with geometric shapes: rectangles and circles.

FLOORSPACE ESTIMATION EXAMPLES:
The final need will depend on your business demands, tasks, and personal preference.

Inspirational floorplan examples:

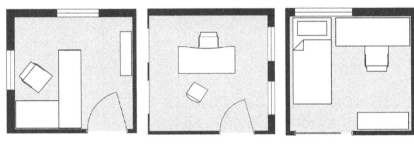

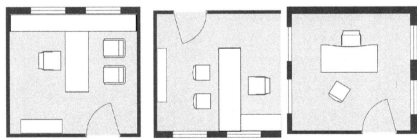

MOST COMMON:

DATA ENTRY CLERK TASKS:
Approximately 100 sqft / 9 sqm

DATA ENTRY & VISITOR / CLIENT ADVISORY:
Approximately 220 sqft / 20 sqm

MY FLOOR PLAN

HOME OFFICE LOCATION CHECKLIST:

- o Floorspace around _____ sqft/m2
- o Privacy
- o Natural light
- o Video call suitable

- o Electricity
- o Internet
- o Heating / AC

STEP 2
COLOR

EEENEY,
MEENEY,
MINEY,
MOE

THE PSYCHOLOGY OF COLOR

NOW, YOU WANT TO LOVE YOUR OFFICE, BE COMFORTABLE, INSPIRED, AND BE SUPER PRODUCTIVE. WHAT COLORS SHOULD YOU SURROUND YOURSELF WITH?

First, let's take a scientific step back; did you know that a human makes an intuitive judgment about a person, object, or also an environment within the first 90 seconds of sight – mainly based on its color?

Color does influence our daily lives in ways we often don't realize – nature has built this into our DNA, and it is the reason why humans have actually survived over thousands of years...

Color can drastically impact our behavior and, therefore, also mood. It can stimulate us to run to safety or to calm down, relax or focus. Retailers, as well as famous restaurants, use this knowledge to optimize the experience for their clients and sales.

DO
USE A COLOR PALETTE; IT WILL MAKE YOUR WORKSPACE FEEL LIKE A MILLION BUCKS;
HOW? SEE MORE ON PAGE 54/55.

COLOR PALETTES

can be inspired by
really anything –
a painting, an object,
a flower bouquet,
a nature scene, and
also can come in any
form.

There is no one magic one-fits-all color palette as it also depends on your personality and preference as well as the tasks, but there are a few hues that are more recommended for the most common corporate office tasks. Let's look at the different characteristics of colors and how they can affect us so you can choose your most successful palette.

A FRESH COAT OF PAINT

A fresh coat of paint is like a spa treatment for your room. It will re-energize the space and set the tone for a new start. If you use another color other than the rest of the room, it will help differentiate the office space and create its own separate working area in a larger room, which is, in fact, also important for your mindset. Now, you enter your work zone physically and mentally.

WHITES & NEUTRALS

- Spaciousness
- Balance
- Tranquility

These colors are great for collaborative spaces and spaces of high focus. The great benefit of such a color palette, it is timeless! This color combination will simply never look outdated. They can also offer great balance to other strong colors.

GREEN

- Peaceful
- Growth
- Health
- Sense of calm

Helps avoid eye fatigue, reduces anxiety – great for workplaces for long hours, lounges, and relaxation areas. Green is a great choice to incorporate in your color palette either as an accent or as one of the main colors – it will definitely support you in maintaining focus and keeping productive.

BLUE

- Trust & honesty
- Communication
- Dependability
- Strength
- Productivity
- Focus
- Stability
- Competence

-> Great for work and collaboration spaces, meeting rooms, and research areas.

Blue is also a great choice to be incorporated into your residential working space - either as an accent color but very well also as the main color covering the walls.

AVOID COMMON MISTAKES AND PITFALLS

RED

Energy, excitement, bold,
and powerful – great for
areas with high activity and
movement like hallways.
It can be tempting and
still look nice, yet it is not
a recommended color
for areas of long hours of
focus and concentration;
it will keep your brain
on edge in fight or flight
mode.

PURPLE / PINK

Feminine, fun, youthful –
frequently used to promote
beauty products.

While it can still look nice,
it is not a recommended
color for long hours of
focus and concentration.

YELLOW

Optimism, warmth, and positivity, inspiring, cheerful – great for very physically active, creative areas, boost energy and creativity.

While yellow is clearly a fun and cheerful color and great for spaces that allow us to recharge energy and be active for a somewhat short period of time, a large amount of very bright yellow will lead to fatigue in no time; Why? The optical physics of light reflection of bright colors results in an excessive amount of processing and therefore, stimulation and irritation of the eyes.

NOW IT'S YOUR TURN

Now that you know what effects colors can have, get some old magazines and scissors, or simply a color printer. And start looking for your ideal color combination:

MAIN COLOR 1 — What is your absolute favorite color? Cut a swatch of it and paste it.

MAIN COLOR 2 — Pick a light neutral color that you like with it; for example, gray, beige, or white.

ACCENT COLORS — Pick 1–3 accent colors: One of them for the metals, which usually comes to a choice of chrome, brass, copper, black or brushed steel, then pick one or two other colors – this can be any you like, and you feel goes well with the main colors.

EXAMPLE COLOR PALETTE

| MAIN COLOR 1: SAGE | MAIN COLOR 2: WHITE | | | |

METALS, BRASS ACCENT COLORS, COGNAC, AND BLACK.

MY HOME OFFICE
COLOR PALETTE

MY MAIN COLOR 1	MY MAIN COLOR 2	MY METAL & ACCENT COLOR

COLOR FOR THE METALS

OPTIONAL

MY FAVOURITE

A NICE NEUTRAL
SUCH AS BEIGE,
GRAY, CREME

THESE GO WELL
TOGETHER WITH
THE MAIN COLORS

STEP 3
FURNITURE

"THE DETAILS ARE
NOT THE DETAILS;
THEY MAKE
THE DESIGN."

Eames

HERE COMES THE SECOND MOST IMPORTANT ASPECT OF YOUR HOME OFFICE

MULTIPLE ASPECTS BELONG TO MAKING THE RIGHT CHOICES WHEN IT COMES TO FURNISHING YOUR WORKSPACE RIGHT: SIZE, PROPORTION, SHAPE, MATERIAL, AND COLOR.

However, the most important aspect is clearly the right chair/desk combination that allows you to sit in good posture.

A lot of the challenges in the home office are actually health related to shoulder, arm, or neck pain due to spending extended periods of time in the wrong posture. The good news: this problem is easy to solve once you know how you should actually be sitting properly.

DO
- ERGONOMIC
- ADJUSTABLE
- SOFT FORMS & SHAPES
- NATURAL MATERIALS
- SPARK JOY

GOOD SEATED POSTURE

Let's look at the right setup for a healthy seated desk work posture top to bottom:

1 HEAD

The screen is one arm's length away from your face – the top of the screen is aligned with your eye level.

2 ARMS

The armrest and desk surface are at the same height, allowing your elbow joints to rest at a 90° angle with constantly shoulders.

3 HANDS

Are as straight as possible at all times, not bent or at an angle. Handsets help avoid strained joints and ligaments of the hands and arms.

4 LEGS

Your knees are at a 90° angle.

5 FEET

Your feet rest firmly and parallel on the floor. If needed, a footrest can help ground the feet.

3

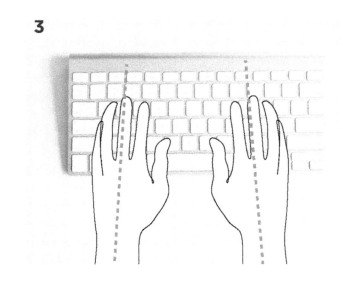

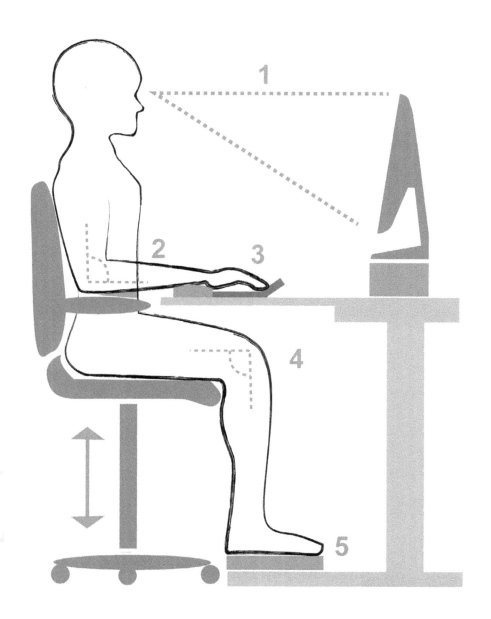

1 A screen / laptop stand can help adjust the screen to the right height.

DESK

In regards to productive office space, it is key to have a desk that suits your needs. Also, it is recommended to choose an actual desk rather than a dining table or side table/sideboard. The overall proportions of other kinds of tables differ clearly from an actual desk and will likely not be ideal for proper posture during seated computer task work over longer periods of time.

However, in the end, it is very much a question of going with what you need to satisfy your requirements and personal preference.

SITTING OR STANDING ?

Some people, in fact, prefer a standing desk. If this is suitable for you, and you have enough space to dedicate an area solely for standing up work – great! Just consider that you may also want to sit down from time to time, so you may have to invest either in an additional seated table space or in a desk that is adjustable.

I ALREADY HAVE A DESK

Can I refurbish a beautiful table I already have? Of course, not a problem! If your desk doesn't offer sufficient height, you can definitely adjust to shorten the legs or accommodate by raising them, for example, with wheels.

DO

CHOOSE A DESK THAT IS LARGE ENOUGH FOR YOUR NEEDS AND A DESIGN YOU LOVE.

I PLAN TO GET A NEW DESK - WHAT SIZE SHOULD IT BE?

HEIGHT   If you have the great liberty to choose a desk with the ideal measurements for your body height, it can be calculated as follows:

$$\text{IDEAL DESK HEIGHT (cm)} = \frac{\text{MY BODY HEIGHT (cm)}}{2.48}$$

SURFACE   First, be really clear on what tasks you need to deliver and calculate the approximate area you need for these. You might start out with something like this (in the end, if you can afford a longer desk – great)

LAPTOP:	20 inches / 50 cm
READING / WRITING:	18 inches / 45 cm
UTENSILS:	12 inches / 20 cm

TOTAL DESK LENGTH
MINIMUM: 50 inches / 115 cm +

CHAIR

If there is one piece to splurge on in your home office, it would be the chair. Ideally, it is good quality, as adjustable and possibly, and you love how it looks and feels to sit in it. But in any case, make sure you have a chair that offers the right seated height. It will be crucial for your posture.

SEAT HEIGHT

If you have the great liberty to choose a chair, the ideal seat height can be calculated as follows:

$$\text{IDEAL SEAT HEIGHT (cm)} = \frac{\text{YOUR BODY HEIGHT (cm)}}{3.72}$$

What about an ergonomic ball or other types of ergonomic seat options? It comes down to your personal preference – the common office chair makes the right posture simply easier to maintain for longer periods of time.

If you setup for longterm work, a convertible standing desk is definitely worth considering as standing up during work can be beneficial for the health of your body as well as feel more productive as studies have shown.

DO
- INVEST IN A GOOD QUALITY CHAIR
- ADJUSTABLE
- NATURAL MATERIALS

SHAPES

To make sure you feel comfortable in your space, it is recommended to not only use furniture with sharp edges and corners but also include soft, round objects – this can be easily done with a chair, curtains, lamps, or decorative accessories. Such as lamps. Also, plants can warm up a stark room that doesn't feel comfortable yet.

MATERIALS

As many neuroscientists have investigated, we can draw a short conclusion: optimized productivity appears in indoor environments that include natural materials such as wood and natural fabrics as these result in an increase of responsiveness and attitude. They will also help prevent neutral colored spaces feel stark and add extra personality and style as well as bring the space to life.

When choosing the types of wood and its colors, it will be helpful to refer back to your previously chosen color scheme.

AVOID COMMON MISTAKES AND PITFALLS

DELIVERY

When ordering furniture, make sure you consider the size of the piece and the available entryways – you do want to avoid it not fitting through the door.

INSTALLATION

If you are renting your place, make sure you are allowed to drill holes or make any changes to the walls.

CHEAP CHAIRS

The chair is almost like a mattress – you will spend so much crucial time on it. Especially, the structure and materials will be worth buying a quality product.

In any case, it makes sense to avoid polyester or plastic seating. You will be drenched in no time, and the materials are likely to wear out/ loose shape rather fast.

SKIPPING THE COLOR PALETTE OR MOOD BOARD

It can be tempting to just buy furniture without preparing a color palette or a mood board first, but your space will lose immediately if you add a piece that doesn't go well with all others.

CLEARANCE AROUND FURNITURE

Make sure to calculate enough room around the furniture to move around, especially behind your chair; 23 inches (60 cm) is the minimum distance required for a chair behind a desk. This would fit a modest-sized chair. For more comfort and to accommodate a bigger office chair, increase the chair clearance to 30 inches (75 cm).

NOW, HOW DO I CHOOSE FURNITURE THAT LOOKS GREAT TOGETHER?

First, you want to choose a "Look & Feel" target for your workspace: Pull out your magazines, catalogs, or the internet to find a home office look you really like, which also uses your step 2 color palette. Cut it or print it out and paste it onto page 70. This is the "Look & Feel" we are going to recreate.

Then, make a furniture list of all the pieces you have and the ones you need to get. Take a picture of the ones you already have and print them out to start your mood board. Now, start searching for the new pieces online or in catalogs using your "Look & Feel" picture to find ones that are similar.

STILL NOT SURE?

OK, LET'S DO ONE TOGETHER

TARGET LOOK & MY STEP 2 COLOR PALETTE

MAIN COLOR 1: SAGE

MAIN COLOR 2: WHITE

THE FURNITURE LIST

HAVE		DETAILS
o	WALL PAINT	Sage green Wall & White Baseboards
o	RODS	White curtain rods

TO GET		DETAILS
o	DESK	natural wodd finish
o	CHAIR	Ergonomic, adjustable, beige leather, chrome finish
o	TASK LAMP	light glamourous finish
o	ACCESSOIRES	Picture frames neutral, Pencil holder white, Vase glass, Chrome details
o	RUG	Offwhite, 160cm x 230cm
o	PLANTERS	Neutral colors
o	CURTAINS	Creme Color

THE FURNITURE PLAN

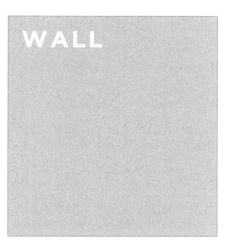

WALL

NOW IT'S YOUR TURN

MY TARGET LOOK AND FEEL
Based on my STEP 2 Color Palette

MY FURNITURE LIST

ITEM   DETAILS

○ _____   _____

○ _____   _____

○ _____   _____

○ _____   _____

○ _____   _____

○ _____   _____

○ _____   _____

○ _____   _____

○ _____   _____

○ _____   _____

○ _____   _____

○ _____   _____

MY FURNITURE PLAN

STEP 4
LIGHTING

DOES IT
REALLY
MAKE
A DIFFERENCE?

IN SHORT - YES!

There have been countless studies conducted with various lighting scenarios over multiple weeks, and the result is: lighting can influence us in many ways. Some even suggest that the right lighting in your office could increase your productivity and sales by 40%!

For once: light impacts the ambiance of a room. And this very ambiance can influence our perception of this space, its smells, its tactile sensations, and even its acoustics. Your goal therefore is to light up the room in such ways you feel absolutely comfortable and welcomed.

DO
Mirrors are a great way to brighten up a darker room, especially when placed across a natural light source.

A ROOM IS NOT A ROOM WITHOUT NATURAL LIGHT

Now considering all this: what is the best lighting setup for my home office?

It is recommended to leverage as much natural lighting as possible. It can reduce stress, anxiety, and very importantly, avoid eye strain. In short, it can improve your productivity and maintain your health.

If there is not enough natural light available in your home office space, you can recreate the right visual ambiance based on changing daylight with adjustable illuminance levels according to task demands and the time of day.

DO
- Natural light
- Sufficient task light
- Layers! The ideal combination of natural, task, and mood lighting will simply make your room.

WORST CASE SCENARIO: BASEMENT

Lighting up a basement can be a daunting exercise, but with a few tricks, you will be done and happy in no time.

First, understand what tasks need to be done and make sure they are all covered with the right light – for these, you will likely use downward facing direct task lamps.

Then add the mood lighting; ambiance lighting, such as linear recessed, indirect strip lighting, or under-cabinet lighting will illuminate all levels of the whole room as well as dark corners and shelves. Just make sure to stick to warm light 3000K or under, and it will create a harmonious ambiance. And the best part about it is those are almost invisible; it will make the room feel as if it is naturally lit up – you might catch yourself looking for the window.

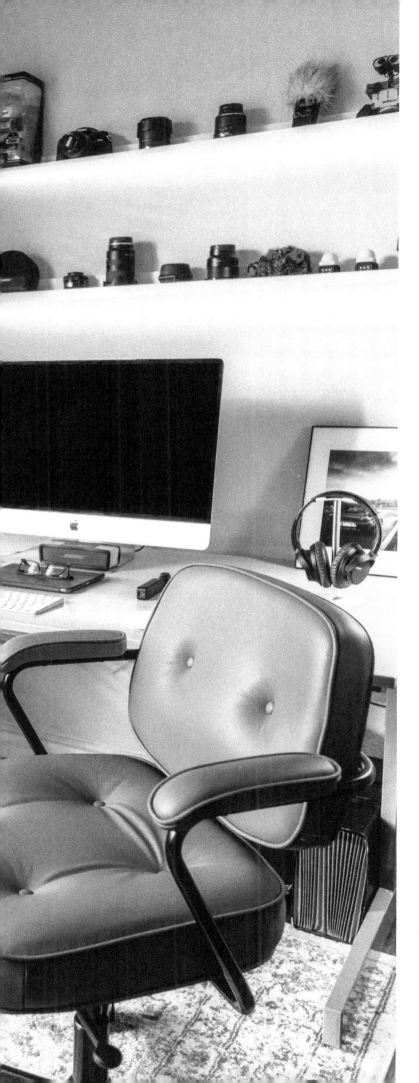

DO

Undershelf strip lights are a great way to brighten dark niche areas while keeping the valuable desk space clutter free.

AVOID COMMON MISTAKES AND PITFALLS

HELP – GLARE IS REAL!

Lighting can cause challenges with glare on screens as well as headaches or eyestrain. Here are a few tips on how we can overcome this:

- Avoid direct overhead lighting such as chandeliers or direct recessed spotlights, which only illuminates the floor.

- Avoid direct reflection: arrange the desk always at an 90° angle to any glass wall or window.

- Add shades to south-facing windows that can help to filter bright light.

- Add an antiglare film to your computer screen.

UP, SIDE, DOWN

When choosing a light, make sure to be aware of the direction the light points to an upward-pointing lamp that will not be suitable as a reading task light. It will make you not feel welcome in your own space and decrease your mood and motivation

AVOID COLD LIGHT

Choose warm temperature light, which has a rather yellow color to it, or around 2700–3000K. Cold (blue) light around 5000K will decrease comfort and is not recommended in home office areas.

AVOID DARKNESS

It won't make you feel welcome in your space and decrease your mood and motivation.

NOW IT'S YOUR TURN

LIGHT UP YOUR LIFE:

A) MAXIMIZE NATURAL LIGHT

The more you can feel connected to the outside, the better: Make the most of the natural light by allowing the light to come in through windows unobstructed by furniture or dark curtains. Light shades can add privacy if needed. You can add windows to the room? Fantastic – go for it!

B) LIGHT UP THE TASK SPACES

Confirm all the tasks you need to do and make sure you plan the appropriate light source for it.
Example: on the desk for reading and writing. Or a reading lamp next to a reading chair.

Also, strip lighting under shelves in cabinets or closets will be very valuable additions.

C) COMPLETE WITH MOOD LIGHTING

Now, we look at the room and see if there are any dark areas left – a floor lamp or table lamp can be great to brighten those.

Especially in workspaces without a lot of natural light, it will be ideal to add indirect lighting from the ceiling to create the sense of daylight.

Overall, the room will feel the best if you have a variety of layers of light coming and going into it.

MY LIGHTING PLAN

WINDOW TREATMENT

o _____ _____

o _____ _____

TASK LIGHTING:

TASK / LOCATION   DETAILS

o _____ _____

o _____ _____

o _____ _____

MOOD LIGHTING:

ITEM   LOCATION DETAILS

o _____ _____

o _____ _____

o _____ _____

o _____ _____

Once you complete this list, you can add those into your floor plan on page 39 by simply drawing circles and cutting and pasting a picture onto your furniture plan on page 78/79.

STEP 5
AIR

DOES THIS
SECTION
SURPRISE YOU?

GOOD!

PRODUCTIVITY IS IN THE AIR

NOW WHY DOES AIR QUALITY MATTER?

It may seem the most logical of all, studies about cognitive function have been exploring the brain functionality in relation to the quality of the indoor environment, and the results are clear; clean air with high levels of oxygen can significantly increase and therefore improve your productivity.

HOW CAN YOU USE THIS KNOWLEDGE IN YOUR HOME?

EASY: keep the oxygen levels high by opening your windows frequently and regularly – 10 minutes of fresh air draft are enough to increase the air quality in a room.

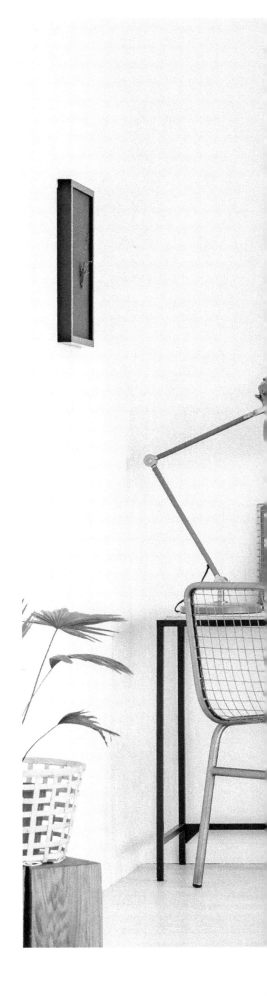

DO

- Air out the room by opening windows regularly.
- Use and change air cleaning filters in your heating/ ac units.
- Use an Air purifier if you live in an area that generally has challenges with clean air.

WHAT A DIFFERENCE A PLANT MAKES

BIOPHILIC DESIGN is on the rise – for good reason: If you add 2–3 plants in your residential workspace, the air will not only be cleaner, as studies show, they also help reduce stress, reduce absenteeism – in short, increase your productivity.

A side benefit of course – they also make the home office more attractive.

If you don't have a green thumb, you can simply choose low maintenance plants that will need possibly a weekly watering and check – the experts in any garden center can help you find the right match, and it doesn't need to be a cactus – there are many ways to keep plants maintenance needs at a minimum.

AVOID COMMON MISTAKES AND PITFALLS

AVOID ALWAYS CLOSED WINDOWS If you keep forgetting to air out the room, set yourself reminders in your calendar.

AVOID HIGH MAINTENANCE PLANTS that need special care or are very sensitive to lighting conditions/temperature – it will not make you very happy if they don't make it past a few weeks in your home – talk to the garden store expert about the conditions in your room. Consider self-watering systems.

AVOID OPEN WINDOWS when you live in an area with bad air quality. In this case it might also make sense to look into getting even more plants – as well as an air purifier. Otherwise of course open them regularly for the additional oxygen boost.

STEP 5
AIR

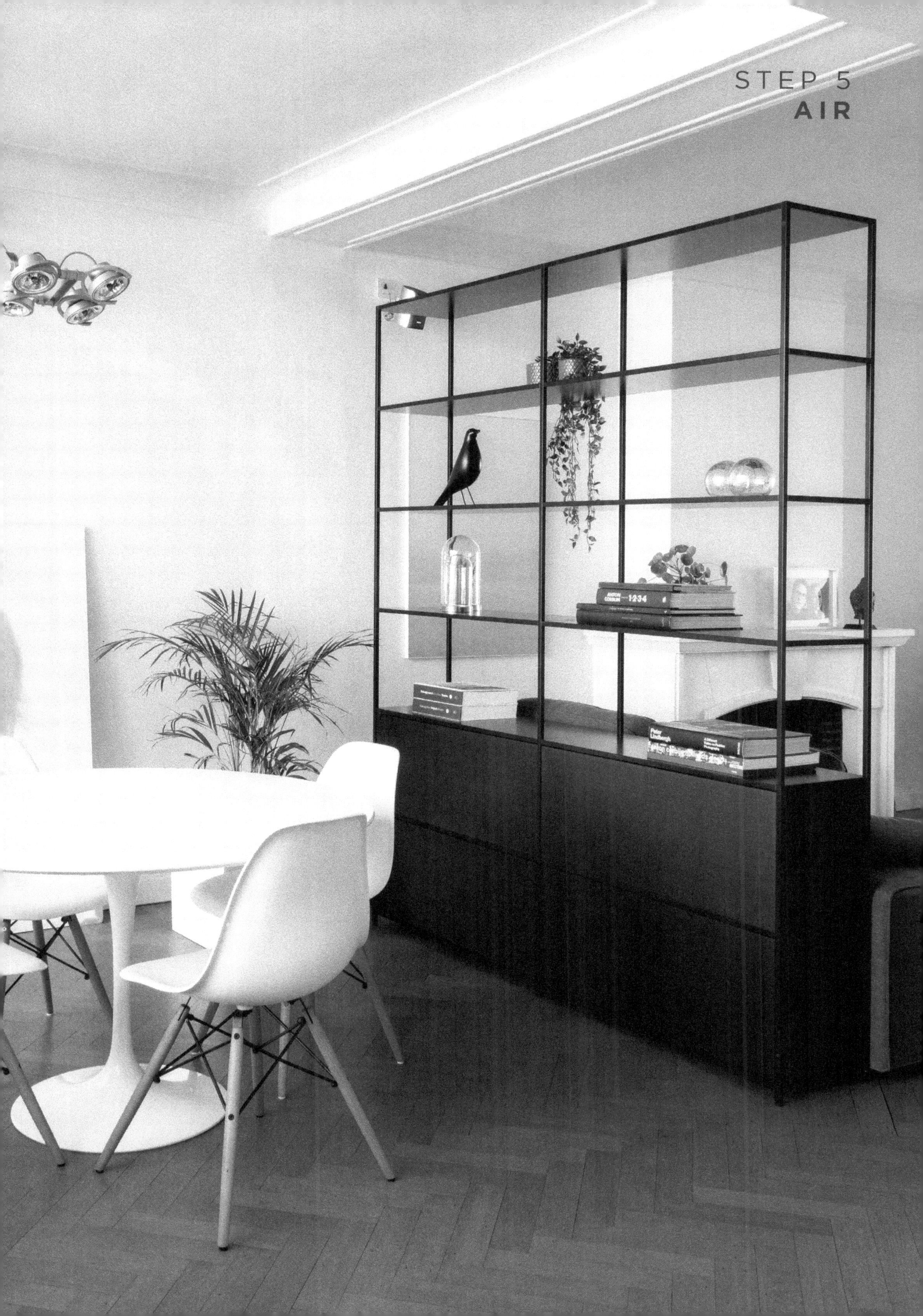

NOW IT'S YOUR TURN

MY AIR OPTIMIZATION PLAN

☐   AIR OUT ROUTINE

☐   SCHEDULED AC/HEATING FILTER CHANGE

☐   PLANTS
If you like, you can cut and paste images onto your furniture plan on pages 78/79

1 _____

2 _____

3 _____

4 _____

_____

_____

_____

MY *ultimate* HOME OFFICE PRODUCTIVITY CHECKLIST

- ☐ **STEP 1 SPACE**
  - ○ LOCATION IDENTIFIED
  - ○ FLOORPLAN CREATED

- ☐ **STEP 2 COLOR**
  - ○ COLOR PALETTE DEFINED

- ☐ **STEP 3 FURNITURE**
  - ○ TARGET LOOK & FEEL CHOSEN
  - ○ MADE A FURNITURE LIST
  - ○ MOODBOARD CREATED
  - ○ PIECES ORDERED

- ☐ **STEP 4 LIGHTING**
  - ○ COMPLETED LIGHTING PLAN
  - ○ LIGHTS CHOSEN
  - ○ LIGHTS ORDERED
  - ○ LIGHTS INSTALLED

- ☐ **STEP 5 AIR**
  - ○ PLANTS PLACED
  - ○ AIR OUT ROUTINE DEFINED
  - ○ AC / FILTER CLEANING SCHEDULED

BONUS
TIPS

STYLE

"THE WAY OF
INTRODUCING
YOURSELF WITHOUT
HAVING TO SPEAK."

Rachel Zoe

WHAT IS STYLE

In design, style is the process of creating something with visual strategic purpose. In our case, it is your residential workspace with the purpose to allow and enable you to maximize your productivity and deliver your very best work.

Naturally, you will be able to do so if you find yourself in a space that makes you feel capable, professional, and simply fantastic.

And the choices we make in regards to any piece we surround ourselves within our home express who we are and what we like.

DO

Treat yourself to nice little details with materials or patterns and textures you adore – it will re-energize you every time you look at them.

WHY DOES IT MATTER ?

Does style even matter or make a difference?

Your style is a reflection of you and your sensorial preferences – meaning if this space matches your own personal style, it will unconsciously inspire and excite you maximizing your productivity – you will do your best work automatically.

Besides that, you will always LOVE to enter your workspace, already starting your workday off in a good mood.

DO
PHOTOS OR ART OF PEOPLE YOU LOVE CAN BE RELAXING AND MOTIVATING.

HOW TO MAKE YOUR ROOM LOOK LIKE IT WAS STYLED BY A PRO

Now, this might sound really too simple to be true but here it goes: you don't actually need to be able to identify and 'name' the various design styles and know which furniture pieces belong to which time period.

The answer is geometrics. Our brains are programmed by nature to find symmetry beautiful – even therapeutic. However, when it comes to interior spaces, it would be very bland and boring if all would simply be symmetrical.

The most pleasing furnished spaces do know how to leverage this effect and break it at the same time while, of course, sticking to a color palette.

Start by arranging all key elements symmetrically and break them up with an off-centered element and odd-numbered decorative elements.

DO
When planning a picture wall, first cut out full-size paper silhouettes of all the frames you have and try the most ideal arrangement.

VIDEO
CONFERENCING

DRESS
HOW YOU WANT TO BE
ADDRESSED

Now you can dress in your best suit – if the visible workspace around you during your video conference is simply a mess, your credibility could suffer or completely distract the audience from your great presentation.

HOW TO MAKE SURE YOUR BACKGROUND LOOKS SIMPLY PROFESSIONAL

The good news: many video conferencing applications have caught onto the problem and are offering different kinds of virtual backgrounds to choose from; you can even upload your own, which are all great options – check the app you use!

However, often we cannot choose the program, so let's anyway make sure our background looks great yes. Here are a few tips.

FOR THE IDEAL VIDEO CONFERENCING SETUP, WE NEED TO CONSIDER FOLLOWING:

LIGHTING

Make sure you sit in front of the brightest light source in the room – ideally, you have as much natural light as possible with a window next to you or in front of you. If the brightest light or a window will be behind you, you will simply be just a silhouette. Also, avoid overhead light, especially if it focuses on a spot behind you.

BACKGROUND

If there is a wall behind you, it shall be plain and monochromatic, and it should be only rather clean and organized items be visible.

Consider any very personal items possibly visible that you don't really want to share. Also, avoid a mirror or a picture frame with highly reflective glass behind you, as it could create glare or possibly reflect another part of the room.

PRIVACY

Consider doors and passageways. If there would be the possibility of someone walking in, you may want to make sure to lock your door. But generally: do not place yourself in front of a door with your back facing the door.

NOISE

If the importance of the call really requires absolute silence, it might be smart you tell the neighbors a day ahead in case they are planning to start some construction. Also, it would be smart to close windows as out of nowhere, there can be this bird showing up or an unexpected truck waiting at a red light.

In an emergency, headphones with integrated microphones can be lifesavers, and for family members, there are now "Do-Not-Disturb" lamps available, so signal when you are on a phone call. Of course an analog sign at the door can also help.

ORGA NIZATION

EVERYTHING NEEDS A HOME

Lucia Gruber

ORGANIZE LIKE A PRO

THE MAGIC is almost too simple to believe, but fact is: if something doesn't have a home, it cannot be stored away.

CREATE A HOME FOR EVERY ITEM

In order to understand your situation, you first need to make a big mess; take out everything and make piles of what belongs together. Then find a place to store it. If there is no proper place yet, make sure to create one.
Leave some empty space for additions that might come and "to sort" drawer always helps to avoid clutter piling up on the desk.

CABLES & WIRES

Attach them with clips along the desk & down the legs to reach the floor invisibly. For Hardwood floors you can get a cable cover in a matching color or get an afforable rug and simply cut a tiny whole in the very spot at the leg to hide the wires under reaching an outlet at the wall.

I HAVE SO MANY BOOKS

but they always look messy. If you have many books there are few tricks to make them look like you are entering an curated museums store: sort them and arrange them in piles by a visual commonality such as color or size and voilà it looks like you had an interior designer stopover.

DO
KEEP THE WORKSPACE ORGANIZED AND CLEAN; COMPARTMENTALIZE AND CREATE AN ACCESSIBLE SPACE FOR EVERYTHING.

ACOUSTICS

IF THOSE
WALLS
DO SPEAK

Noise is one of the most common stressors creating noise fatigue, which leads to a drastic drop in productivity. We may be able to choose a location that can enable us to control the acoustics we are exposed to; however, some really don't have a choice. And on top, there can be unexpected construction below or above us...

In this case, noise cancellation headphones can be an essential support to blend out any acoustic stress factor.

However, when choosing your home office workspace, do consider the location also for its soundproof qualities!

In case you have noisy wood flooring, and you are not the only person residing in your home during your working hours, considering textile floor coverings of any sort can be of great help.

DO

CHOOSE A SPACE
IN WHICH YOU CAN
INFLUENCE THE
SOUND
ENVIRONMENT.

BEFO
A
Inspir

RE &

FTER

ation

AND YES,
YOU CAN DO
IT TOO!

PROMOTED

This stunning upgrade by the so very talented Noelle Flint proofs that sticking to a color palette in combination with the right furniture placement will make all the difference in the world.

BEFORE

THE ELEPHANT IN THE ROOM

You really looked everywhere in your home for some working space but there simply is none? Look again!

BEFORE

AFTER

WALK-IN CLOSET WONDER

You don't need a lot of space; focus on a few pieces of furniture in the right size in combination with the right lighting and magic happens – like this beautiful collaboration of Sisalla Interior Design and Plane Architectural Joinery.

ATTIC
TURNED
LUX

If your only option is a tiny, dark room under the roof, don't despair: Lighting is key in dark spaces, and you can still have all the lux you want, even on a budget.

BEFORE

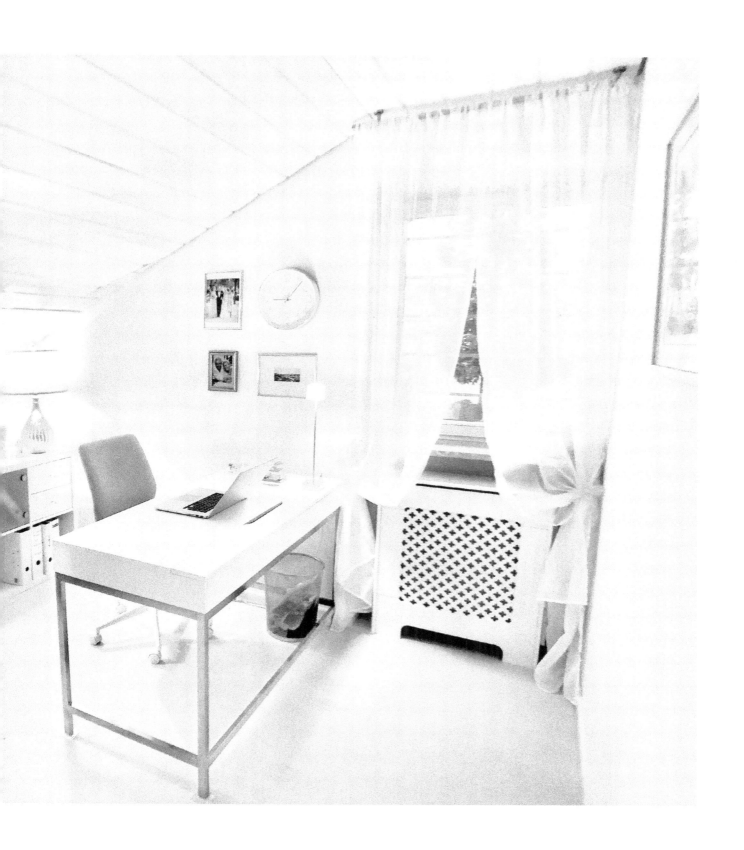

WHAT A DIFFERENCE NATURE MAKES

This simulation showcases
how natural, warm materials
and a few accessories can
easily make a great difference.

BEFORE

LIGHT UP

This simulation showcases how a little addition of layered lighting can make a big difference especially in rooms with little natural daylight. The more indirect lighting the better.

BEFORE

NATURALLY NEUTRAL

With complimenting shapes & textures, a choiceful color palette and the right scale of furniture this office became an oasis for a music lover.

BEFORE

INDEX

IMAGE CREDITS

Back Cover Top left to bottom right:
All floorplans by Lucia Gruber.

Printed in the USA
CPSIA information can be obtained
at www.ICGtesting.com
LVHW061351130224
771561LV00024B/259